CW00383614

The Parents' and Catechists' Companion

to *Loved and Forgiven*
and *Meet Christ with Joy*

The Parents' and Catechists' Companion

to *Loved and Forgiven*
and *Meet Christ with Joy*

Joan Brown SND

kevin
mayhew

kevin
mayhew

First published in Great Britain in 1999 by Kevin Mayhew Ltd
Buxhall, Stowmarket, Suffolk IP14 3BW
Tel: +44 (0) 1449 737978 Fax: +44 (0) 1449 737834
E-mail: info@kevinmayhewltd.com

www.kevinmayhew.com

9 8 7 6 5 4 3 2 1

ISBN 978 1 84003 474 5
Catalogue No. 1500322

Illustrated by Natalie Bould
Cover design by Jonathan Stroulger
Edited by Helen Elliot
Typeset by Kevin Whomes

Printed and bound in Great Britain

Contents

Loved and Forgiven

	Children's book page	Page
Introduction		11
UNIT 1: WELCOME		
Home session 1	2	13
Group session 1	3	14
Home session 2	4 - 5	15
Group session 2	6 - 7	16
Home session 3	6 - 7	18
UNIT 2: MYSELF		
Group session 3	8 - 12	19
Home session 4	8 - 12	20
UNIT 3: LISTENING		
Group session 4	13 - 15	23
Home session 5	13 - 15	25
Group session 5	16 - 17	26
Home session 6	16 - 17	28
UNIT 4: REMEMBER		
Group session 6	17 - 20	29
Home session 7	18 - 22	33
UNIT 5: HOME REJOICING		
Parents' and catechists' notes		35
Group session 7	23 - 25	37
Home session 8	26	41

Meet Christ with Joy

	Children's book page	Page
Introduction		45
UNIT 1: COMMUNITY		
Parents' and catechists' notes		
Preparing for the celebration of enrolment		47
Belonging together as a community		48
Belonging to a family		48
Group session 1		
Gathering and welcoming the children		50
Home session 1		
Families	2 - 7	52
Parents' and catechists' notes		
Baptism		54
Group session 2		
Belonging to my Christian family	6, 7	55
Home session 2		
Family life	8, 9	57
UNIT 2: PRAYER		
Parents' and catechists' notes		59
Group session 3		
Praying in the heart	8 - 10	61
Home session 3		
Family prayers	10 - 11	63
Group session 4		
Mass prayers	11	64
Home session 4		
Family love	13,12	66
UNIT 3: GOOD NEWS		
Parents' and catechists' notes		
A story to share		67

Group session 5
A story to share   16   68

Home session 5
A story to share   14 - 17   70
The lost sheep   71
The widow's mite   72
The loaves and fishes   73
The good Samaritan   74
Jesus washes his disciples' feet   75

UNIT 4: CELEBRATION

Parents' and catechists' notes   77

Group session 6
Celebration   18, 19, 21   79

Home session 6
Celebration   18, 20, 21   80

UNIT 5: REMEMBERING

Parents' and catechists' notes   81

Group session 7
We give God thanks and praise   24, 25   83

Home session 7
Heaven and earth are full of God's glory   23, 26   85

Group session 8
A special meal   22   86

Group session 9
Through Jesus Christ our Lord   28, 29   88

Home session 8
Through Jesus Christ our Lord   27   90

Home session 9
We remember   30, 31   91

Acknowledgements   93

About the author

Joan Brown is a Sister of Notre Dame de Namur. She has extensive experience in teaching and catechesis in both Britain and Africa. She has been involved in parish-based Catechetical programmes and liturgy work and also served as RE Advisor to the Diocese of Arundel & Brighton. A trained spiritual director and retreat giver, Sr Joan now runs her own small house of prayer as well as continuing her writing.

Loved and Forgiven

Who among you with a hundred sheep, losing one,
would not leave the ninety-nine in the wilderness and
go after the missing one until it was found?
And when found would you not joyfully carry it on your
shoulders and call together your neighbours and friends
when you got home and say, 'Rejoice with me,
I have found my sheep that was lost'. In the same way,
I tell you, there will be more rejoicing in heaven over one
repentant sinner than over ninety-nine virtuous who
have no need of repentance.

Or again, what woman with ten coins would not,
if she lost one, light a lamp, sweep out the house and
search thoroughly until she found it. And when she
found it, call together her friends and neighbours?
She would say, 'Rejoice with me, I have found the money
that I lost'. In the same way, I tell you, there is rejoicing
among the angels of God over one repentant sinner.

Adapted from Luke 15:4-10

Introduction

Originally the title for this book was going to be 'Home Rejoicing'. Reading the two stories from St Luke's gospel (opposite) explains why. When we celebrate the Sacrament of Reconciliation we celebrate the end of a journey; a journey on which we are carried in the loving arms of God, from whom we walked away. And there is rejoicing among the angels in heaven over this homecoming. This is the great joy of repentance.

But what does it mean, repent? Images of hanging one's head in shame accompany our understanding of repentance; regretting one's actions, self reproach, sorrow, remorse; a distant scene of rejoicing angels. Repentance or contrition is a gift of the Holy Spirit. It is the love of God above all else: not shame or regret or remorse or self reproach, but the love of God above all else. This is perfect contrition. However, like the prodigal son sitting starving in the pigsty, our contrition is usually a realisation of the ugliness of sin and of the state in which we find ourselves, or the fear of what might eventually happen to us. And so, prompted by the Holy Spirit, we get up and go to seek forgiveness. We begin the journey.

I do not know who it was who said, 'To err is human, to forgive is divine'. Only God can forgive sin. Only humans can sin. We call this sacrament the Sacrament of Reconciliation because it pours out on the sinner the love of God who reconciles, as the father in Luke 15 pours out unconditional love when his lost son returns. 'While he was still a long way off, his father saw him and was moved with pity. He ran to the boy, clasped him in his arms and kissed him tenderly.'

> The whole purpose and effect of this sacrament is reconciliation with God. The Sacrament of Reconciliation with God brings about true 'spiritual resurrection', restoration of the dignity and blessings of the life of the children of God, the most precious of which is friendship with God. 1468*

> Reconciliation with God leads to other reconciliations. The forgiven penitent is reconciled with self,

with family and friends, with the Church and with all creation 1469

The Sacrament of Reconciliation is also called the Sacrament of Conversion, Penance, Confession, Forgiveness, each of these names telling us something of the nature of this healing sacrament.

'Loved and Forgiven' leads the children through the new rite of the Sacrament of Reconciliation. Each unit takes one aspect of the rite as children experience it in their natural day-to-day living. Hopefully the children will gradually be able to relate their natural understanding and experience of welcome, listening, remembering and rejoicing to the sacramental celebration of reconciliation, and also come to a deeper understanding and appreciation of themselves and their value in the eyes of God.

*Paragraph numbers refer to the Catechism of the Catholic Church.

Unit 1: Welcome

Home session 1

Begin by giving your child time to explore the book and tell you what they think about it. What do they like best about it?

Tell them that 'Loved and Forgiven' is a special book because it will help them to get ready to meet Jesus in a special way. It will help them to prepare to meet him in a sacrament – the Sacrament of Reconciliation.

'Sacrament' and 'Reconciliation'. What do these two big words mean? What does your child think they mean?

'Sacrament' means a sign – for example, a hand-shake is a sign of friendship.

Think of some more signs and what they mean.

A sacrament is a sign that Jesus is here – it is a holy sign. It is a sign of Jesus and us meeting.

'Reconciliation' means being friends again.

Why do people stop being friends?

How do they become friends again?

How do they show they are friends again?

The Sacrament of Reconciliation is a holy sign that we are friends with Jesus and each other.

◆ Open the book 'Loved and Forgiven' at the pink page facing page 3.

Read together what is written on this page. Start with the red-coloured words.

Why is this book such a special book?

Who is this book helping you to prepare to meet?

Now help your child to fill the pink page.

Group session 1

Materials: a welcoming name card for each child
some drinks and biscuits for the children to share

Introduce the children to the catechists.

Invite the children to say their names, where they live, schools they attend, their favourite things, hobbies.

◆ Page 3: invite the children to describe what is on this page.

Where can they write their name?

Ask the children to write their names.

How do we show people that they are welcome?

Did the children feel welcome when they arrived at the session?

What made them feel welcome?

How does it feel to be welcomed?

How does it feel to be unwelcome?

Encourage the children to give examples of people who make them feel welcome.

Where do they feel most welcome?

How would they like to fill in page 3, with writing or drawings or both, or a story?

Ask the children to bring their baptism candles, photographs and other baptismal mementoes they may have to the next group session.

Home session 2

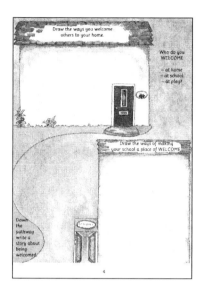

◆ Page 4: read through the page with your child and then let them write the number of your house on the house and the name of their school on the school.

This page is about how we make others welcome at home . . . at school . . . at play.

Ways we make others feel welcome at home

What does it ask you to do on the roof of the house?

Who are the people you welcome into your home?

In what ways do you show them they are welcome?

Ways we make others feel welcome at school

What does it say on the roof of the school?

Who do you welcome into your school?

How do you show visitors to your school that they are welcome?

Ways we make others feel welcome at play

When the house and school are full of welcomes look at what is written on the grassy patch.

Help your child to write a story about being welcomed. It can be a true story or an imaginary one.

◆ Page 5: complete this 'wonderful world' page.

Read the invitation from God and then let your child write their name on it, very beautifully, perhaps with a gold or silver glitter pen.

Group session 2

Materials: a table for each child with a candle or night-light

children's name cards from session 1

large candle

Bible

flowers

dish of water

matches and taper

Welcome the children.

Look at the work they have completed on pages 3, 4 and 5.

Invite the children to show and tell the group about the baptism mementoes they have brought.

◆ Read through page 6 with the children.

Tell them that this is a very special page with another 'welcome' from God.

How did God welcome them on page 3?

How did God welcome them on page 5?

How is God welcoming them now on page 6?

God has welcomed us with love. God has welcomed us into our beautiful world and now we are being welcomed into God's very own family.

What is there to see on page 6?

The candle is a sign of Jesus, the light of the world. We are asked to keep the light of Jesus burning brightly in our lives by sharing the love of Jesus with everyone we meet.

The dove is a sign of the Holy Spirit to remind us that we have been given new life in baptism through water and the Holy Spirit.

There is a place to stick a picture of your baptism, or you at the age you were at your baptism.

Below the candle are the promises of baptism with another place to write your name.

Read through these promises with the children.

In whom do we say we believe?

Who do we say God is?

Who do we say Jesus is?

Relate God the Creator to the wonderful world page (page 5).

What do the children know about Jesus?

What is their favourite story about Jesus?

What have they learnt about the Holy Spirit on page 6?

The Holy Catholic Church is the sign of God's new life on earth given to us through water and the Holy Spirit.

The communion of saints is all the people everywhere who live with God's new life.

Life everlasting is the new life that never ends.

The children could draw a picture to illustrate these beliefs.

◆ *Page 7: complete the session with the Celebration of Loving Welcome.*

Have a 'baptism' cake to share.

Home session 3

◆ Complete page 6. Perhaps your child could use a gold or special pen to fill in their details.

There is a space for your child to stick or draw a picture of their baptism.

Show your child their baptismal candle and baptismal certificate.

Tell your child:

where they were baptised

the name of the Church

the priest who baptised them

their godparents' names

anything else you can remember about the day.

Show them any photographs you have, any cards or keepsakes, perhaps even their baptismal gown.

Say the promises of baptism together.

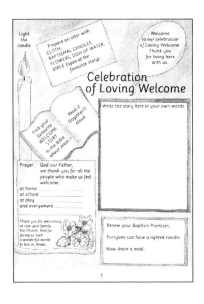

◆ Fill in page 7.

Help your child to find their own favourite story about Jesus in the Bible and to write it in the space provided.

As a family you might like to have your own Celebration of Loving Welcome.

Unit 2: Myself

Group session 3

Materials: bathroom scales

mirror

wall height chart

large cut-out bathroom scales

large cut-out shoe or foot

children's and catechists' names printed clearly on cards

clothes peg for each person

one or two autobiographies of famous people

Welcome the children.

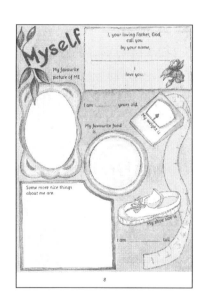

◆ Page 8: ask the children what the message from God is on the card.

Play a game. Describe a person in the room by their appearance. The one who guesses fastens the person's name on with a clothes peg and takes the next turn to describe someone. Continue until all have been described and name-pegged.

It would be very difficult if every time we wanted to speak about someone or call someone we had to do it by describing them. 'Will the boy with brown straight hair, green jumper, grey trousers, two ears and a nose please come for his book?'

Our names are very special. We were given our names by our families. We were called by our names in baptism when we became God's beloved children. God knows each one us by our name.

Together read the message on the flowered card.

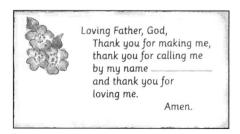

◆ Tell the children that pages 8, 9, 10, 11 and 12 are going to be their life story, just like those of the people in books.

Home session 4

Help your child to complete pages 8, 9, 10, 11 and 12. Again give them a special pen with which to fill in their name.

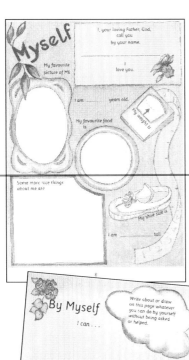

◆ On page 8 tell your child what you and your family consider to be their best qualities.

Is there anything else your child might like to add to this page, such as a favourite colour, book, animal, hobby, game, person, their fingerprints? They might like to make a poster with some of this information on for the group display.

On another sheet of paper your child might like to make a beautiful picture of their name and put their photograph with it. These name pictures can then be used in the parish display.

◆ Page 9 is a fun page.

Ask your child to read what it says in the cloud about this page.

Help them to discover some of the things they can now do by themselves that perhaps they could not do a year ago, like tying shoelaces, tidying their things away, maybe reading.

Fill the page with writing, drawings, photos and so on.

◆ Page 10: ask your child what is different about this page from the ones they have been doing.

This page is about your child and their family.

What name has to be written in the box on this page?

How is your child going to write your family name?

What is a family name?

Why do we call it a family name?

It is the name you share with other members of your family. You might like to draw a little family tree with your child, showing the other members of your family who share your family name.

Find a family photo for the frame or compose a picture by cutting pictures of family members from different photos.

Fill the 'with my family on holiday' space with a written account, a drawing or a holiday snap.

Draw what you most like doing with your family. Everyone in the family can be invited to share in this activity. Tell your children what you most enjoy doing with them.

Last of all on page 10 there are some pages of the calendar to fill in. What are special days in your family: anniversaries, birthdays, baptism days, first communion days? Stick extra pages on to the calendar if enough have not been provided.

◆ Now you have arrived at page 11.

What is this page about?

It is about friends. Who are your child's friends?

Tell your child about your friends, past and present.

What do they like best about their friends?

Friends can be young, old, in the middle.

Can your child show these qualities in the pictures they draw of their friends?

Use the rest of page 11 to draw or write about some happy times with friends.

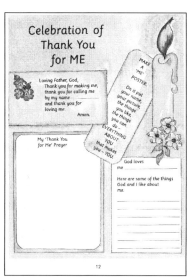

◆ Page 12 is a celebration page.

Ask your child what is being celebrated on this page.

Read through the page together.

What is your child's message to God on the flowered card?

For the 'thank you for me' prayer, look back at what your child likes most about themselves (page 8).

Help them to recall the wonderful things they are able to do, and their special gifts (page 9).

Make a 'ME' poster (page 8).

In the white space, fill in some of the lovely things God likes about them.

You are now ready for your celebration.

Loving Father, God,
Thank you for making me,
thank you for calling me
by my name
and thank you for
loving me.
                    Amen.

With your child, prepare a table with a candle and flowers and some of your child's favourite things.

When all are gathered, light the candle, and sing one of your child's favourite songs.

Let them say the prayer from the flowered card on page 12.

All share some of the things you like about your child and each other.

Let your child say their 'thank you for me' prayer.

Have something special for tea.

Unit 3: Listening

Group session 4

Materials: objects which make different sounds, e.g.

bell

whistle

stones in a tin or jar

bottle of water

Bible

candle

taper and matches

Welcome the children.

Begin the session by being very quiet and still, with eyes closed, or backs turned, listening to the sounds made by the different objects.

How many objects can the children identify by their sounds?

Listen to the sounds in and around the room. How many can the children hear and identify?

◆ Page 13: if the children could hear the sounds made by the objects in these pictures, what would they hear? Encourage the children to make the sounds.

Listening is very important. If we do not listen carefully we can get the wrong message or miss an important message.

Give the children the following, or some other, message and then ask for a volunteer(s) to repeat it: **'Today is an important day because it is the day when we come together to learn more about Jesus.'**

What messages do the children listen to at home, at school?

When do they sometimes not listen and with what results?

23

Today we are going to listen to a story told by Jesus. It is a story about a sheep who was glad she listened.

◆ Read the story on page 14. Begin by counting the sheep up to ninety-nine.

Ask the children what the story was about.

What did they like best about it?

What did the man know about his hundred sheep?

What did the man think might have happened to the lost sheep?

How did the man manage to find the lost sheep?

How did the sheep help itself to be found?

Mime the story with the children.

Choose a shepherd, sheep, lost sheep, river, mountain peak, wolves, thief. All can be rejoicing friends.

Have any of the children ever been lost?

What did it feel like to be found?

◆ Page 15 is a 'pretend' page.

In these stories told by Jesus, what or who are the children asked to pretend to be?

Read the stories to find out who God is pretending to be.

What kind of ending do these stories have?

◆ Conclude the session by praying together the prayer from page 12.

Loving Father, God,
Thank you for making me,
thank you for calling me
by my name _____
and thank you for
loving me.
Amen.

Home session 5

◆ Read the black text on page 13 with your child.

Write the names of all the sounds you can both hear.

With how many sounds can you fill this page?

What is your child's favourite sound and why?

Write this on page 13.

Share with your child your favourite sound.

◆ Read the story of the found sheep on page 14 as a bedtime story with your child.

Perhaps your child might like to draw some pictures of the adventures of the lost sheep, how it became lost, how it escaped and some of the terrible things that might have happened to it.

How did the story end?

Invite your child to draw a wonderful picture of the man rejoicing with his found sheep.

◆ Page 15 is a pretend page.

Read what you are asked to pretend. Your child might like to draw a picture story rather than write.

You need your Bible for the next part of this page. In the Bible find the three stories from St Luke's Gospel. Read the stories with your child again, perhaps as bedtime stories.

In each story what is lost and what is found?

Again there is some pretending to do. You might like to help your child pretend by giving them the opportunity to act out the stories. Other children or family members might like to join in the hide-and-seek games.

Be sure to explain to your child what it feels like to be found/saved.

Group session 5

Materials: Bible

double-folded heart-shaped cut-out for each child

candle

matches and taper

Welcome the children.

Give the children the opportunity to share the work they have completed on pages 13 and 15.

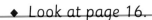

◆ Look at page 16.

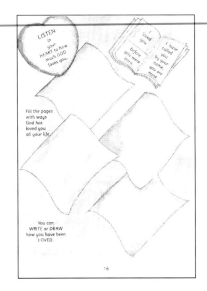

Ask the children to find where they are being asked to listen today.

What is the message they will hear if they listen in their hearts?

For how long has God loved us?

God loved us before anyone knew what we were going to be like.

God loved us before we grew up to be . . . (describe the children's physical appearances one by one).

When the group recognise and name the child described, continue by saying: 'and God has loved N . . . since before he/she was born and will love N . . . for ever.'

Continue until all the group has been described by the leader or catechist.

◆ On page 16 the children write their names in the 'book'.

Discuss with the children the many different ways they have been loved by God all their lives:

being born into a beautiful world

having a family to care for, feed and clothe them

being taught to read and write

having food to eat

being able to run, jump, play

having friends to play with

being called to be baptised into God's family

being called to be Jesus' friend in the Sacrament of Reconciliation.

Read some of the children's favourite stories from the Bible about God's love.

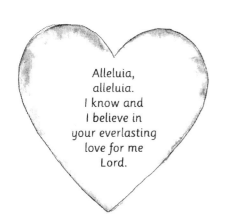

Alleluia, alleluia. I know and I believe in your everlasting love for me Lord.

◆ From page 17, give each child a heart-shaped booklet.

On the front cover let the children copy (or have already printed) the text from the heart shape on page 17, 'Alleluia, alleluia . . .'

On each of the following pages in the 'heart book', ask the children to write a way in which they know and believe in God's everlasting love for them. Books can have card covers which the children can decorate.

Conclude the session by praying together the Alleluia prayer from the heart shape on page 17.

Home session 6

Begin by sharing with your child what they have written in their heart-shaped book.

◆ Page 16: help your child to fill the 'pages' in, very beautifully, with different ways in which they have experienced how God loves them.

◆ Page 17 is a Celebration of Listening.

Help your child to compose a prayer of thanksgiving for all the ways in which they are loved.

Write this in the blue box on page 17.

Help your child to make a list of all the people who love them.

Then write the names in the pink box on page 17.

Use the Celebration of Listening on page 17 as a bedtime prayer with your children. For this celebration you need your Bible and your child's and your family's favourite Bible stories.

Unit 4: Remember

Group session 6

Materials: candle

    matches and taper

    Bible

    crucifix

    brightly coloured balloon for each child, personalise these by writing or labelling each balloon with a child's name.

Welcome the children.

◆ Page 17: begin this session with a Celebration of Listening.

Gather the children into a circle.

Light the candle.

Leader: God loves us all very much. For each one God has a special message of love.

    Address each child by name saying:

    I loved you, N . . ., before you were born. I have called you by your name. You are mine.

Leader: Each one of us is now invited to say 'thank you' to God for one of the ways we know God loves us.

    Each child in turn quotes from one of their 'pages' on page 16.

    After each quote:

All: **Thank you, God, for loving N . . .**

Leader: Let us now welcome God's holy word of love with the Alleluia.

All: **Alleluia, alleluia. I know and I believe in your everlasting love for me, Lord.**

Read a short Gospel story of God's love.

Repeat the Alleluia.

Close with a suitable song or hymn.

◆ Page 18 is about remembering.

Invite the children to explain what the word 'REMEMBER' means to them.

What kind of things can they remember?

How many things can they remember?

What is a happy memory?

What is an unhappy memory?

How do the children on page 18 look?

Give each child a balloon with their name on.

Ask the children to remember a time when they loved and cared and shared at home to make their family happy.

When they have remembered, the children blow a puff of air into their balloons.

Now remember a time at school when they loved and shared and cared to make their friends happy.

Blow a second puff of air into the balloon.

In this way, blow 3 or 4 more happy 'rememberings' into the balloons, keeping the air in the balloons.

The balloons are now full of love.

They are light. They can float.

They make us happy. We enjoy playing with them.

◆ When everyone has nice big balloons, turn to page 19.

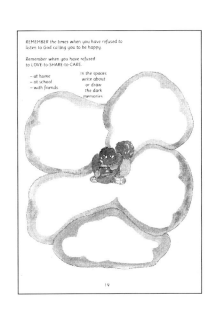

Ask the children how this page is different from page 18.

How are the children different?

What might they have been doing?

This page asks us to remember the times when we have made other people unhappy; times when we have not been loving and caring and sharing.

What do the children think is the opposite of loving, of caring, of sharing? Be more explicit than not loving, not caring, not sharing.

Invite the children to remember a time when they made someone unhappy at home by being hurtful, mean or selfish.

When the children have remembered they let a puff of air escape from their balloons.

Now ask the children to remember a time at school when they fought or spoilt things for their friends and made them unhappy.

Then let a puff of air out of the balloon.

The children continue with more memories of making others and themselves unhappy until the balloons are empty of air.

Show the children two balloons, one empty of air and one full.

Tell the children that, like the balloons, we can be small and shrivelled up by fighting and meanness, jealousy and lies, cheating, bad temper and spitefulness – the children can add examples – or we can be filled with love – the love which makes us and everybody around us full of happiness.

We can be helpful, polite, kind to little brothers and sisters, truthful, thoughtful; ready to share our things. The children can add examples and, as they do so, they can blow up their balloons again, then fasten them securely to keep the air in.

Whether we are big, fat, floaty balloons, or little, shrivelled, flat balloons, God will never, ever stop loving us. God will always help us to blow the breath of love back in.

◆ Look at page 20.

Seat the children in a circle.

Address each child individually and say: **'Remember, Jesus always loves you, N . . . Jesus always calls your name and is always there to help you to say sorry.'**

Light the candle and place it beside the crucifix.

Complete the session by reading the story below of the good thief, adapted from St Luke 23:33-34, 39-43.

Just before Jesus died on the cross he did something very wonderful. On the crosses on either side of

REMEMBER –
Jesus always loves you _____
Jesus always calls your name
Jesus is always there for you.
Jesus will always help you
to say
SORRY
And to come back
to him.

WRITE YOUR OWN PRAYER
OF SORROW HERE.

20

Jesus were two thieves. One of them began to mock Jesus. 'If you are who you say you are, why don't you work one of your miracles and save yourself and us as well?' The other thief spoke up and told him off. 'Have you no fear of God at all? We were given the same sentence as Jesus, but we deserved it. We are paying for our wickedness. Jesus has not done anything wrong. Jesus,' he said, 'remember me when you come into your kingdom.' And Jesus said, 'I promise you, today you will be with me in paradise.'

Home session 7

◆ Look at page 18 with your child.

Help your child to remember some happy times they have shared with family and friends at home and at school.

What made these times happy?

Fill the spaces with drawings or written descriptions of these happy times, including specific things that made them happy.

◆ How is page 19 different from page 18?

Is it a happy page?

What is not happy about it?

Has your child ever felt like the children on this page?

Why, when do they feel like this?

Help your child to draw or write about some of these times.

◆ Is page 20 a happy or a sad page?

Of which story are we reminded on this page?

Just as the shepherd went out to search for the lost sheep, so God will always come looking for us – wanting to help us no matter how sad or miserable we are, or how far away we have strayed. No person or place is ever too dark for God's love to light up.

What does the word 'SORRY' mean to your child?

◆ In the space on page 20 help your child to write their own prayer of sorrow.

◆ Fill page 21 together with ways they can give love and happiness to their family and friends.

Use the 'Remember' prayers on pages 21 and 22 and your child's own 'Sorry' prayer each night with your child at bedtime.

◆ Enjoy the Celebration of Remembering on page 22 with your child.

Unit 5: Home rejoicing

Parents' and catechists' notes

What are your childhood memories of the celebration of the Sacrament of Penance and Reconciliation? What memories and understanding of this sacrament do you want your children to retain? Imagine yourself as a little child of seven or eight years of age celebrating this sacrament for the first time. What help do you need?

The Celebration of the Sacrament of Penance

All sacraments are celebrations of the wonderful works of God on our behalf. In her liturgy the Church celebrates and proclaims the work of Christ our Lord in redeeming us through his passion, death and resurrection and giving perfect glory to God. 'Seated at the right hand of God' and pouring out the Holy Spirit on his Body, the Church, Christ now acts through the sacraments he instituted to communicate his gift. ADAPTED 1067, 1084

Sin is an offence against God, a breakdown of our relationship with God. It is also a breakdown of our relationship with the Church. Conversion, therefore, requires both God's forgiveness and reconciliation with the Church, which is expressed and accomplished by the celebration of the Sacrament of Penance and Reconciliation. ADAPTED 1440

To confess our sin sets us free to be reconciled with others and makes a new future possible. ADAPTED 1445

Confession to a priest is an essential part of this sacrament. Christ entrusted the power to forgive sins to his apostles and their successors. ADAPTED 1456, 1441, 1461

In celebrating the Sacrament of Penance the priest is fulfilling the ministry of the Good Shepherd seeking the lost sheep, or the Good Samaritan, binding up the wounds of the injured. The priest is the sign and instrument of God's merciful love for the sinner, the loving Father who greets the prodigal with outstretched arms and a kiss. ADAPTED 1465

The elements of the Sacrament of Penance and Reconciliation are:

- the greeting and blessing from the priest
- the reading from the Word of God to illuminate the conscience and arouse contrition for sin (the reading may precede the sacramental celebration)
- advice and encouragement by the priest
- the confession of sin by the penitent to the priest
- the giving of and acceptance of a penance
- the priest's absolution
- a prayer of thanksgiving and praise and dismissal with the blessing of the priest. ADAPTED 1480

The Sacrament of Penance may also be celebrated in a communal service in which we prepare ourselves together for confession and give thanks together for the forgiveness received. ADAPTED 1482

Group session 7

Materials: Bible

crucifix

candle

matches and taper

a few blown-up balloons

Gather the children and seat them in a circle.

Light the candle and place beside the crucifix.

Leader: *making the sign of the cross*

Welcome. In the name of the Father and of the Son and of the Holy Spirit.

Then, naming each child individually, proceed as follows:

Leader: Welcome, N . . .

All: **In the name of the Father and of the Son and of the Holy Spirit.**

and repeat until all the children have been named and welcomed.

Each child now speaks their name and age:

My name is . . . and I am . . . years old.

◆ Page 24: listen and remember.

Listen

We now listen to God's message of love.

Read the story of Zacchaeus, the man who welcomed Jesus joyfully into his home and found his life changed, adapted from St Luke 19:1-10 (see page 39).

Remember

Who did Zacchaeus want to see?

What did Jesus ask him to do?

What did Zacchaeus remember?

Zacchaeus remembered all the times he had been mean and selfish; the times when he had been greedy; the times when he had cheated and stolen from the poor people. He made up his mind, with the help of Jesus, to change his life. Instead of being mean and selfish and greedy, he would be generous and caring. Instead of cheating and stealing from poor people, he would help them and give them half his money.

How do we want Jesus to help us to change?

Are we ever mean and selfish and greedy? When, where, with whom?

Do we ever steal or cheat?

Do we ever want or take more than our fair share?

Do we bully children smaller than we are?

Do we ever tell lies?

Give the children time to sit quietly to remember the 'flat balloon' times in their lives and to say sorry to Jesus in their hearts.

◆ Together pray the prayer of sorrow from page 24.

◆ Page 25: rejoice

Children all make the sign of the cross.

Leader: God our loving Father forgives us because Jesus died and rose again for us and sent his Holy Spirit to be with us for the forgiveness of sins.

All pray: Loving God,
we praise and thank you;
you are great and wonderful.
Thank you for sending Jesus to help us.
Thank you for sending your Holy Spirit
to bring us forgiveness and peace.
Thank you that we can come home to you
rejoicing. Amen.

◆ Page 23: complete this session by giving each child a personalised invitation card. Include the date on which the child is to celebrate this sacrament.

Group session 7: Luke 19:1-10

The story of Zacchaeus

One day Jesus came to a town called Jericho.

Where is Jericho? Is it near here?

Has anyone here been to Jericho?

Jericho is the town whose walls came tumbling down a long time ago, a long time before even Jesus was born. Seven holy men, with seven trumpets, marched round Jericho for seven days, and on the seventh day when they blew their trumpets the walls came tumbling down. Ever since then Jericho was a very special town for the Jewish people. On this particular day we are hearing about, Jesus came to Jericho and was walking through the town.

What would happen here in . . . (name your town) if someone famous was visiting, like . . . (invite the children to name a famous person)?

When the people of Jericho heard that Jesus was in town they came running out of their houses and shops to see him. A great crowd gathered round him.

Is there anyone here called Zacchaeus?

Does anyone have a brother or cousin or grandad called Zacchaeus?

A man whose name was Zacchaeus heard that Jesus was in town. What kind of man was this Zacchaeus? Well, he was very, very rich. But what did he do for a living, to get very, very rich? He collected tax money in fact he was the chief collector of tax money. Everyone has to pay tax to the government of their country to help pay for things like roads, hospitals and schools. Sometimes people have to pay a lot of tax, like nearly half of all the money they earn. Zacchaeus collected the tax money from the Jewish people, but he collected it for the Roman government, who paid him well but did not use the money to help the Jewish people. So everyone hated Zacchaeus for helping the Romans.

When Zacchaeus heard Jesus was in town he was curious and wanted to see Jesus for himself. As well as being very, very rich, Zacchaeus was also a little man, and because he was so short he could not see Jesus for the crowd.

Has anyone here been in a big crowd and not been able to see anything?

How have you been helped to see over a crowd?

Zacchaeus had a bright idea. He ran ahead of the crowd, spotted a sycamore tree and climbed up it. Now he would have a grand view when Jesus passed beneath him. Zacchaeus was in for a big surprise because, when Jesus reached the sycamore tree, he stopped underneath it and looked up at Zacchaeus, the very, very rich man, perched there in the branches, and said to him: 'Zacchaeus, come down. Hurry, because I must stay in your house today.'

Imagine someone very famous like . . . (name of famous person) coming to . . . (your town) and saying, '. . . (name of child), I must stay in your house today.' (Repeat, using names of all or several of the children, depending on the size of the group.)

How did Zacchaeus feel? He might have felt . . .?

But he did not feel silly or foolish or embarrassed about being spotted up the tree; no, he was delighted, and he hurried down and welcomed Jesus joyfully into his home.

He welcomed Jesus in all the lovely welcoming ways you wrote about at the beginning of your book. What might some of these ways be?

Some people complained when they saw what was happening. 'Jesus has gone to stay at a sinner's house,' they said. They were jealous. But Zacchaeus had changed, because he had met Jesus. He said to Jesus, 'Look, sir, I am going to give half of everything I have to the poor.'

If the children were to give half of everything they have away, what would that mean? Half their toys . . . clothes . . . pocket money?

Zacchaeus also said, 'If I have cheated anybody I will pay back four times the amount.'

In practical terms, this means making up four times over.

And Jesus said, 'Today Zacchaeus is saved'.

Home session 8

Retell the story of Zacchaeus to your child as a bedtime story.

Zacchaeus was a small man. He was in the same situation as a child; he could not see above the crowd. He climbed a tree to get a better view.

Who did he want to see?

When Jesus passed beneath the tree, he looked up at Zacchaeus. People usually looked down on him, but Jesus looked up to him and even asked to visit his house. Zacchaeus ran home rejoicing. He confessed his bad way of living. What was that?

He resolved to change his life. How?

What did Jesus say he had brought to the house of Zacchaeus?

◆ *On page 26, help your child to write or draw how, like Zacchaeus, they want to change and try to be more like Jesus, at home and with their friends.*

Meet Christ with Joy

Introduction

There was once a time when life was more predictable than it is today. It had a fairly set pattern as season followed season. In those once-upon-a-time days, nothing ever seemed to change and when people came to church they knew what to expect.

The Liturgical year, with its seasons of purple and green and white, and its festivals of red and gold, flowed through the months. The blue of Mary days, processions and saints' days, litanies, devotions and blessings all had place and meaning as the rhythm of life and the changing seasons of the year were gathered into worship.

In the pace of life today the seasons blur into one another. Feasts and festivals come and go uncelebrated, unnoticed, apart from the commercialising of Christmas and Easter. Even before the Christmas decorations are taken down summer holidays are being planned and booked. As the gulf between life and liturgy grows ever wider, the links between life and what we give worth to, what we worship, are lost; we are in danger of being left with empty ritual and meaningless symbol.

Concerned about this situation, the Church issued the 'Directory on Children's Masses', encouraging us to 'draw upon all that is human' to help children to come to a fuller understanding of liturgy and in particular the Eucharist – this in order to enable children to participate more fully and meaningfully in the celebration.

> All those who are concerned with the education of children should work and plan together to ensure that the children, besides having some idea of God and the supernatural, should also, in proportion to their years and degree of maturity as persons, have some experience of those human values which are involved in Eucharistic celebration: for example, acting together as a community; exchanging greetings; the capacity to listen, to forgive and to ask forgiveness; the expression of gratitude; the experience of symbolic actions, conviviality and festive celebration.

> The aim of Eucharistic catechesis will therefore be to cultivate the human values, so that the children's appreciation of Christian values and the celebration of the Mystery of Christ will keep pace with their age and psychological and social condition.
> DCM n.9

In 'Meet Christ with Joy' the human value of acting together as a community is developed through the themes of 'My Family/My Christian Family'; 'Family Life/With God's Family at Church'; and 'Family Celebrations'. 'Welcoming and Greeting' come naturally into these themes, each theme relating the child's understanding of life to liturgical celebration.

The theme of 'Listening' introduces the children to Scripture and to the Liturgy of the Word at Mass.

In the theme of 'Giving Thanks', the children express gratitude for who they are, for the whole of life and acknowledge everything as a gift from God. In this way the children are led into the heart of the Eucharist, the great act of thanksgiving and the wonderful work of our Redemption.

> . . . It is in the liturgy, especially in the divine sacrifice of the Eucharist, that 'the work of our redemption is accomplished', and it is through the Eucharist that the faithful are enabled to express in their lives and manifest to others the mystery of Christ and the real nature of the true Church.
> Sacrosanctum Concilium 2

Each Sunday, when we gather as a community to celebrate the Eucharist, we proclaim to each other and to the world the saving power of the death and resurrection of Christ. For the Church to come alive therefore, the Eucharist must be meaningful in our lives and in the lives of our children. Renewed and refreshed by our participation in the sacrifice of the Mass, it is our mission to go forth in Christ to bring the good news to the world – to 'Go in peace to love and to serve the Lord', and so to bring the mystery we have celebrated into our daily lives and into the life of every person we meet.

Unit 1: Community

Parents' and catechists' notes

Preparing for the Celebration of Enrolment

Celebrating the enrolment of candidates preparing for their first celebration of Holy Communion reminds us that, as human beings, we live in a world of time. As the writer of the book of Ecclesiastes reminds us, 'For everything there is a season, and a time for every matter under heaven'. However, we are seldom present to our season or to the present moment. We are on to the next thing, into tomorrow, before today is half begun. By celebrating the enrolment of candidates into the time of preparation we are celebrating the 'now', the present moment in the lives of these children, this stage in their journey of faith. We are saying that what is happening to these candidates now is important and that we want to mark this time in a special way, to make it significant. We want to take time over this in order that the candidates and the community become fully aware of what is happening, focus in on this moment of time, marking not only a new stage in the faith journey of the candidates, but also that of the community which celebrates this new life springing up in its midst.

Faith is a lifelong journey and baptism, confirmation and eucharist, the sacraments of Christian initiation, are the foundation of every Christian life. Already members of the Body of Christ born into the Church and raised to the dignity of the royal priesthood by baptism, candidates for eucharist are now asking publicly to participate with the whole community in the Lord's own sacrifice by means of the communion under the appearance of bread and wine.

This Celebration of Enrolment reminds us that we do not live our faith alone. Faith draws us into a community of believers, all of whom must be committed to the initiation of their candidates. Eucharistic catechesis therefore is given in the name of the community who first lovingly and willingly welcomed these candidates into their midst in baptism.

During the Celebration of Enrolment the children receive their copies of 'Meet Christ with Joy'.

Belonging together as a community

> I have called you by your name, you are mine.
> Isaiah 43:2

To name something, be it a teddy bear, a house or a person, creates in us a feeling of responsibility for it. The relationship between us and that which we name changes. A bond forms between us. From now on we belong together.

In the book of Isaiah we have the beautiful example of God saying just this to the chosen people, the people called by name, people who need never fear because they are redeemed, called by name to be God's very own. Nothing will be harmful to them, rivers, seas will not drown them; fires, flames will not burn them.

In St Matthew's Gospel Jesus tells us not to worry about our life and what we are to eat and drink and wear, because our heavenly Father knows all our needs. We have nothing to fear from tomorrow (Matthew 6:31-33). And in Matthew 10:28-31 we are told that God knows each one intimately, even to the number of hairs on our heads. We must not be afraid. Nothing can happen to us without our heavenly Father knowing. Truly, named for God in baptism, each of us is precious in God's eyes, honoured and loved.

> You are mine, O my child, I am your Father,
> and I love you with a perfect love.
> I have called you by your name; you are mine.

> Adapted from the hymn 'Do not be afraid', Gerard Markland,
> © 1978 Kevin Mayhew Ltd

Belonging to a family

The family is the place where children first receive their faith, education and values. It is with the family that children first share meals, learn to celebrate and to pray. From their parents children hear their first Bible stories. In the home they see the crucifix, statues, holy pictures, the rosary and prayer books. As the family presented their children for baptism, it is the family who now presents them for their first celebration of communion and, supported by the parish, helps their children to prepare for this celebration.

The liturgical formation of children is based on, and cannot be separated from, human values. Eucharistic catechesis should develop these values. It is within the family that the greatest influence lies and where these values are first imbibed. Welcoming, exchanging greetings, listening, seeking and granting forgiveness, saying thank you, sharing meals and festive celebrations, experiencing symbolic action, all are part of family life and important if children are to be helped to come to a religious understanding of these actions and values when we use them in worship.

Group session 1: Gathering and welcoming the children

Materials: large candle drawn on a sheet of paper or card

gold marker pen(s)

strips of coloured paper

glue

card and coloured pens for each child to make their name card for the Celebration of Enrolment

Begin the session with children and catechists seated in a circle.

Tell the children that everyone has a name. Our names are very important; they are the way in which we know and remember each other. Everyone has a special family name which we share with the family to which we belong. Invite each child and catechist to say their family name aloud.

Everyone has a special Christian name, the name by which God knows them. We were given this name when we were baptised. Because we are baptised, we belong to God's Christian family. Our baptismal name is our Christian name. God knows each one of us by our name. Invite each one to say their Christian name aloud. How many names can each person now remember?

Do the children know the 'stories' of their Christian names? Who chose their names? Why were they given these names? Are they named for someone in their families? What do they know about this person? Are they named after a saint? What do they know about the saint?

Catechists might share one or two stories about their names.

Light a candle.

Leader: These children, very precious friends of God, will soon be called by name to God's table to prepare to receive Jesus in Holy Communion.

All hold hands.

Leader: Lord Jesus, help these children to prepare with love for your coming to them in Holy Communion.

Unless the group is too big, pray for each child individually by name.

Leader: Lord Jesus help N . . . to prepare with love for your coming to her/him in Holy Communion.

At our baptism we were given a lighted candle, a sign of Jesus Christ, the light of the world. We were asked to keep it burning brightly by believing in Jesus. Ask the children to name something that we believe about Jesus.

Invite the children to write their Christian names in gold in and around the card 'candle flame' as a sign that their candles are still burning brightly because they believe in Jesus.

The children write their Christian names on a card and decorate them, ready for the celebration of enrolment. Describe to the children what will happen at the enrolment celebration.

Each person now writes their name on one of the strips of coloured paper.

The strips are then fastened together to form a chain.

All hold hands and sing 'Bind us together, Lord'.

Home session 1: Families

◆ Page 2: 'Meet Christ with Joy'

Read through this page with your child.

Help your child to write her/his name on the line provided and the names of other family members on the lines below.

◆ Read page 3 and discuss the different ways of being family.

Help your child to draw some of the different ways of being family.

Talk with your child about your own special family and your special way of being family. Help your child to draw your special way of being family.

Invite your child to tell you what they think is the nicest quality about each person in the family picture they have drawn including themselves. What do they like best about belonging to their special family?

BELONG – how does your child understand the meaning of 'belong'?

Help your child to draw, colour and decorate the word BELONG.

◆ Page 4: My family

Explain the meaning of 'family name'.

Give your child paper and coloured pens to draw and colour your family name.

Names of my family.

Perhaps compile a simple family tree.

Choose a family photo to stick in the book.

My family's special days.

These can be any days which your family keeps as special birthdays, anniversaries, Mothering Sunday, Father's Day.

◆ Page 5: My Christian name

Tell your child why you chose their Christian name. Help your child to make a beautiful picture of their Christian name and write it on the baptismal font. If it is the name of a saint, find out about the saint.

Tell your child the date of their baptism. Show them their baptismal certificate and candle. Tell your child what happened to them during their baptism and how they behaved.

Complete page 5.

◆ Page 6: My Christian family

Help your child to choose a photograph of their baptism for this page, or a photo of them at the age they were at their baptism.

Fill in the name of the church where they were baptised, who the priest was, and the names of their godparents. Tell your child why you invited these people to be godparents.

Were there other people present at the baptism? Look at any photographs you may have of the celebration.

Tell your child that you took them to church to be baptised because you wanted them to have the wonderful gift of being a child of God. You wanted them to belong to God's family in a very special way and have Jesus for their brother.

Complete page 6.

◆ Page 7: Family prayer

This page is self-explanatory.

If possible, invite your child's godparents to celebrate with you and have a nice family meal afterwards.

Parents' and catechists' notes

Baptism

Baptism, the sacrament of faith, is the basis of the whole Christian life. It is birth into the new life in Christ, the gateway to life in the Spirit, and it gives access to all other sacraments.

In Baptism we are freed from sin and reborn with new life as children of God and temples of the Holy Spirit. Incorporated into Christ and his Church, we are made sharers in the priesthood of Christ, consecrated for Christian worship. 1213, 1272, 1273*

This sacrament is called baptism from the Greek 'baptizien' which means to plunge or to immerse. Plunging, or immersing in water, is the central rite by which baptism is carried out. To be plunged or immersed in water symbolises the catechumen's death and burial into Christ's death from which s/he rises up with him, as 'a new creature'. 1214

The celebration of baptism begins with the signing of the baptismal candidate with the sign of the cross of Christ, signifying the grace of redemption which Christ won for us by his death on the cross. The candidate and the gathered community are then enlightened by the proclamation of the Word of God. This is followed by the laying-on of hands or anointing the candidate with the oil of catechumens. Immediately before the baptism the power of the Holy Spirit is called down upon the water, so that those to be baptised in it may be 'born of water and the Spirit'. The candidate is then immersed three times in the water and baptised in the name of the Father and of the Son and of the Holy Spirit. Next the newly baptised is anointed with the oil of chrism, signifying the gift of the Holy Spirit to the newly baptised. Being clothed in a white garment symbolises that the newly baptised has 'put on', is risen with, Christ. Finally, the presentation of the candle, lit from the Easter candle, signifies that Christ has enlightened the newly baptised. In Christ the newly baptised is the 'light of the world'. 1235-1243

*Paragraph numbers refer to the Catechism of the Catholic Church.

Group session 2: Belonging to my Christian family

Materials: sheet of A4 paper for each child, can be coloured, rolled to form a scroll and with text as follows . . .

Beloved Child

I call you by name

. . . .

You are mine. (◆ see page 6)

gold pen for children to write their name on their scroll.

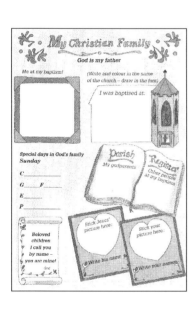

◆ Invite the children to share the work they have completed at home (pages 2 to 5).

Help the children to understand what it means to belong to the Christian family; that their family brought them to church to be baptised because they wanted them to be God's children, brothers and sisters of Jesus and of each other as members of God's Christian family, the Church.

Take the children into church to see the baptismal font and the paschal candle. Let each one bless themselves with water from the font saying: 'In the name of the Father and of the Son and of the Holy Spirit.' We are baptised in the name of God, Father, Son and Holy Spirit.

Show the children the oil of chrism with which they were anointed at baptism. Anoint the children with some oil (not the chrism) saying: 'I anoint you with oil in the name of Jesus, Our Lord. May his power make you strong to be like him.'

Light the paschal candle, saying: 'This is the light of Christ. May we keep it burning brightly. May we always live as children of the light.'

Explain how the paschal candle is lighted on Holy Saturday, the day after Good Friday, and that it stands for Jesus, risen from the dead, the light of the world. Explain how the candle they were given when they were baptised is a miniature paschal candle

and represents the light of Jesus lighting up their lives, their faith in Jesus.

◆ *Recite together the baptismal promises from page 7.*

Show the children the parish register. Tell them that the Christian name by which they were called when they were baptised is written in the parish register of the church of their baptism. This is the name by which God knows them and calls them.

The day we were baptised into the family of God is one of the special days of our lives.

Give each child one of the scrolls to complete.

To conclude this session pray together, holding hands, the great prayer of God's family which Jesus taught us, 'Our Father . . .'.

Home session 2: Family life

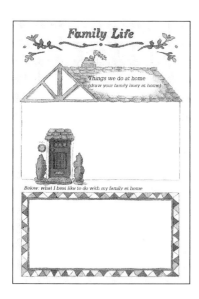

◆ Page 8: Things we do at home

With your child identify the welcoming moments in your day at home.

What greetings might you exchange with each other daily? on special occasions? with other people?

When, to whom, to what and where do you listen?

To what do you and your child most like to listen? Why?

When, to whom and why might you say 'sorry'?

When and why do you say 'thank you'?

Where and when and why do you share meals?

What does your child enjoy most, and least, about family meals?

Think about some of your family celebrations. Which is your child's favourite? What is special to each celebration (cakes, decorations, rings, cards, clothes)?

Complete page 8.

◆ Page 9: With God's family at church

Things we do at church

Page 9 complements page 8.

Who welcomes us when we go to church and when? You may be welcomed by parishioners when you arrive at church.

The celebrant welcomes us at the beginning of Mass. Find out what these words of welcome are.

When do we say sorry at Mass?

What words do we use?

When, to whom and to what do we listen at Mass?

Show your child the readings in a missal or on a missalette.

When, why and for what do we say thank you at Mass?

Find a Sunday or feast day preface and read it to

your child. Perhaps count how many different ones there are.

When do we share a meal?

What do we call sharing a meal at church?

What is your child's favourite church celebration?

Complete page 9.

Unit 2: Prayer

Parents' and catechists' notes

It is vitally important, as we accompany our children on their developing journey of faith, that we help them, through prayer, to come to know personally the God who loves them.

Short moments of reflective silence are more essential than ever for children in the noisy world in which we live today. Children can be introduced to prayerful silence through Scripture-based prayer reflections. In this form of prayerful silence children can meet Jesus, who is at the heart of their faith experience, in their own deep and personal way. They can experience the close sharing of friends; a time to be with the One they know who loves them.

Prayer is God's gift to us. It enables us to raise our minds and hearts to God, to ask good things from God, and to set our hearts on God.

In St Luke's Gospel chapter 1, we read, 'Once, Jesus was in a certain place praying; when he had finished, one of his disciples said, "Lord, teach us to pray, just as John taught his disciples".' It is important that parents teach their children how to use God's gift of prayer, just as John and Jesus taught their disciples to pray.

We are told that the Christian family is the first place where children learn to pray. It is parents who teach children simple morning and night-time prayers; who show them how to make the sign of the Cross; how to bless themselves with holy water on entering the church; how to genuflect; who teach them to bless the food before meals. Through simple words, gestures and actions, children come to realise that it is the whole person who prays. But unless these words, gestures and actions come from a heart set on God, they have no meaning.

> Prayer is the life of the new heart. It ought to animate us at every moment. Often we forget God who is our life, our all. 2697

> The Eucharist contains and expresses all forms of prayer. It is the sacrifice of praise. 2643

'Prayer' is the name we give to the many and varied ways in which we communicate with God:

– Prayers of blessing and appreciation of God and God's wonderful world.

– Adoration, awe and wonder before the God who made us.

– Petition, expressing our need of God.

– Contrition, trusting in God's loving mercy.

– Thanksgiving, at all times and in all things, remembering God's gifts.

– Praise embraces all the other forms of prayer, for praise quite simply gives glory to God because God is. Praise is the prayer of the pure of heart who see God.

Group session 3:
Praying in the heart

Materials: prepare a table with prayer artefacts, e.g.

    rosary

    holy water stoup

    prayer books

    crucifix

    candles

    holy pictures

◆ Invite the children to share the work they have completed at home (pages 8-9).

Family prayers.

Invite the children to describe what they think prayer is. Ask them what prayers they know.

When do they pray? Why do they pray?

Where do they pray? To whom do they pray?

How many different places to pray in can they think of?

Have they a favourite prayer, a favourite place to pray?

Show the children the different objects connected with prayer on the table.

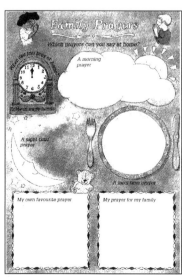

◆ Page 10: Discuss the questions on this page with the children.

Praying in your heart.

Seat all the children comfortably, perhaps on rugs or cushions; when all are settled read aloud 'The First Disciples', John 1:35-39:

One day, Jesus walked beside the river Jordan. John the Baptist, his cousin, was standing with two friends. 'Look!' said John, 'there is Jesus, the lamb of God'. When they heard this John's two friends followed Jesus. Jesus turned round and saw them following him. 'What do you want?' he asked them. 'We want to know where you live,' they replied.

'Come and see,' said Jesus. So they went with Jesus and saw where he lived, and they stayed with him the rest of that day.

Invite the children to sit quietly and imagine themselves as one of the friends following Jesus to his house.

Then ask them to draw a picture of themselves with Jesus in his house. In the picture, write what they and Jesus say to each other. Tell the children they can visit Jesus in his 'house' and talk to him at any time.

Home session 3: Family prayers

◆ On pages 10 and 11, look at prayer in the home and in the Mass.

With your child discuss the questions:

When and where can you pray at home?

What is your child's understanding of prayer?

A morning prayer

Compose or find a morning prayer. What might your child want to pray at the beginning of each new day?

A night-time prayer

Compose or find a night-time prayer. What might your child want to pray each night?

A meal time prayer

How do we praise and thank God at meal times?

Encourage your child to write their favourite prayer in the space provided. Perhaps give them a special pen to write it with.

With your child, compose a prayer for your family.

Write it in the space provided.

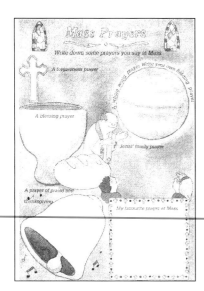

Group session 4: Mass prayers

◆ Invite the children to share the work they have completed on page 10.

◆ On page 11, how many different ways of praying can the children find?

Sorrow. Asking. Blessing. Praising.

Invite the children to make up simple examples of these ways of praying, perhaps by drawing pictures of themselves or other people praying in this way, and writing the prayer being prayed in the picture.

Prayers of forgiveness at Mass

Penitential Rite . . . 'I confess . . .' 'Lord, have mercy . . .' Absolution.

'Lamb of God . . .' 'Lord I am not worthy'.

Prayers of asking at Mass

Prayer of the Faithful.

Prayers for the needs of the whole world.

Explain how these are invitations to pray for a special need, for example 'Let us pray for the sick', 'Let us ask the Lord to . . .'.

Blessing prayer

Show the children hosts, ciborium, wine, chalice.

Teach them the prayer of blessing, 'Blessed are you, Lord God of all creation . . .' Read a final blessing.

Prayer of praise

Final doxology pronounced in praise of God: 'through him, with him, in him . . .'. When we say this prayer we remember that through, with and in Jesus we give praise, honour and glory to God for ever.

Jesus' family prayer

The 'Our Father'. Jesus gave this prayer to his friends when they asked him to teach them how to pray. Read Luke 11:1-4.

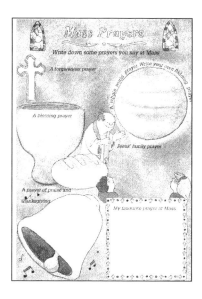

◆ On page 11: children can either copy the prayers into the spaces provided or stick in prayers printed out.

Children could complete the page by writing their favourite Mass prayer in the space on the right.

Complete the session by gathering the children together around a focal point, such as a picture of Jesus; bread and wine; open Bible; and pray a forgiveness prayer, some bidding prayers, the 'Our Father' and the final doxology.

Home session 4: Family love

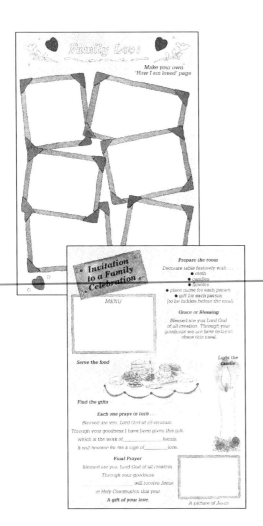

◆ Page 13

Help your child to make their own 'How I am loved' page.

Discuss with your child what kind of pictures would show the different ways their family shows love for them.

Draw these pictures in the spaces provided or use photographs.

◆ Page 12

Prepare and celebrate the Family Celebration.

Decide the menu with your child.

The gifts for each person can be home made; a card, home-made sweets, a picture drawn by your child, a prayer. You might like to invite your child's godparents.

Unit 3: Good news

Parents' and catechists' notes

A story to share

For most of his life Jesus lived an ordinary everyday life at home with his family, with its daily routine and its ups and downs, like the rest of us. In living this life Jesus experienced and came to understand love – love of parents, relatives, friends; what it feels like to love and to be loved and to know himself as beloved of God.

In the midst of a loving family children come to faith, come to know God and come to know themselves as lovable and beloved of God.

> Sacred Scripture is the speech of God as it is put down in writing under the breath of the Holy Spirit.
> Dei Verbum 9

> Through all the words of Scripture, God speaks only one single Word. This Word is a complete expression of God. This same Word became flesh and lived among us. This is why we venerate Scripture in the same way that we venerate the Lord's Body. The Church presents the faithful with the bread of life from the one table of God's Word and Christ's Body. 102

> Christian faith, however, is not a 'religion of the book'. Christianity is the religion of the 'living Word of God'. This Word became flesh and at the heart of the Scriptures are the four Gospels, our principal source for discovering the life and teaching of the Word incarnate, our Saviour, Jesus Christ. In the Gospels we meet and relate to a person, to Jesus, the Word of God. 125

We approach Scripture, God's holy Word, with awe and reverence. We listen with our hearts to the words of Scripture because we believe we are listening to Jesus, who is calling us to follow him and who says to us, 'As the Father has loved me, so have I loved you; abide in my love'. And again: 'This is my commandment, that you love one another as I have loved you.' John 15:9, 12

Group session 5:
A story to share

Materials: prepare a table of the Word – on a stand covered with a cloth decorated with flowers and candle, place a copy of the Bible

Bible for each catechist

Begin this session by gathering the children around the table of the Word. Explain that in church the Bible has its own special place called the lectern. Today we have prepared a special place for the Bible.

The Bible is the greatest book ever written. It is the book of God's word, telling us the story of God's great love for us. Show the children how the Bible has two parts: the Old Testament, or the story of God's love for people before Jesus was born; and the New Testament, the story of how Jesus lived on earth, what he taught us about God's love for us, and how he died to save us.

Let us now listen to God's holy Word.

Light the candles.

Take the Bible from the stand and hold it up.

Reader: A reading from the Holy Gospel given to us by St Luke (10:38-42).

All respond: Glory to you, Lord.

(with the thumb sign a small cross on forehead, lips, heart.)

Lord, open my mind to hear your word.
Open my lips to speak your word.
Open my heart that I may love and live your word.

(At the end of the Gospel hold up the Bible . . .)

Reader: This is the Gospel of the Lord.

All: Praise to you, Lord Jesus Christ.

How well have we listened?

Name the people in the story.

Who welcomed Jesus into her house?

Who sat at the Lord's feet and listened to him?

Who worried about many things?

Who did Jesus say had made the best choice?

What was Mary's choice?

When do we make the choice of listening to Jesus?

Tell the children that we listen to God's holy Word every time we celebrate Mass.

◆ Page 16 introduces the children to the Liturgy of the Word.

Take the children into the church and show them the lectern and the lectionary.

Give each child an opportunity to stand at the lectern and to read from the lectionary (a short sentence only).

Home session 5:
A story to share

♦ Page 14: God loves us

Help the children to find the New Testament stories to which the Bible references on page 14 relate.

Read them together (see pages 71-75).

What is the message in the stories?

How does your child feel about the message?

♦ Page 15 Our love for one another

In what ways are pages 14 and 15 alike and in what ways are they different?

Who are the people today who are loving and caring like the shepherd?

Or like the woman who gave away her last coin?

Or the little boy who gave away his dinner?

Or the good Samaritan?

♦ Complete page 16 to show how what we listen to with love at church we put into action at home, at school, at play.

♦ Page 17. Draw your child's attention to the Liturgy of the Word at Mass.

Explain that the first reading is usually from the Old Testament, the Word of God spoken to the people of Israel.

In the Psalm we respond to God's Word and make it our own.

The second reading is from the New Testament and tells us how the first Christians listened to God's Word and lived it in their lives.

The Alleluia acclaims that Jesus Christ is present in the Gospel.

We stand to greet Jesus in the Gospel.

A story to share: Luke 15:4-7

The lost sheep

Begin by asking which children have a pet – a dog, cat, hamster rabbit, perhaps a goldfish.

What names have the children given their pets?

How do they care for their pets?

If, on arriving home from school one day, they discovered only an empty cage or basket, and their pet missing, how would they feel? (This may have been an experience for some children.)

What would they do?

When the pet was found, how would they feel?

Why would they feel this way?

Once Jesus told us a story about a man who had a hundred pets. He loved them all so much he could not bear it if one was lost. It was the story of the lost sheep. Then Jesus asked: 'Which of you, if you had a hundred sheep and lost one, would not leave the ninety-nine on the hillside and go searching for the missing one until it was found? And when it was found, carry it home on your shoulders? And then you would say to your friends, "Rejoice with me, I have found my sheep that was lost." '

How would we answer Jesus' question?

Each one of us is very special to God. God loves and cares for each one of us. Among all the millions of people in the world God knows and loves and cares about . . . (name each child in turn). God would miss us if we were not there – if we were lost.

Invite the children to sit quietly and to think about God loving and caring for them.

A story to share: Luke 21:1-4

The widow's mite

Have a pocket money discussion with the children. What is pocket money? What is it meant for? Who gives it? Why? What is it used for?

What is the difference between pocket money and housekeeping money? What are savings? What are they for?

Today Jesus tells us a story about a woman who had no pocket money and no savings. All she had was her housekeeping money. Let us listen to what she did with it.

One day Jesus was teaching the people in the Temple in Jerusalem. Some of his disciple friends were with him. They could see many people coming in and going out of the Temple and some of the people were putting gifts of money into the treasury. Some of the rich people were giving a lot of money. Then Jesus saw a poor woman. She was a widow so had no husband to earn money for her or take care of her. She was all alone. She came up to the treasury and put two small coins into it. Jesus turned to his friends and said, 'Did you see the poor widow placing her offering into the treasury? I tell you, she has put in more than all the rich people together. They put in their spare money, but she put in everything she has to live on.'

It was as though the woman put in her pocket money, her housekeeping money and all her savings. She had nothing left. Not even enough to buy a bit of bread. She believed in God's love for her. She believed in God's care for her. Jesus noticed what she did, and it has never been forgotten.

What do the children think about this story? What is it saying to them?

Invite the children to sit quietly and think of a way to show their belief in God's love and care for them.

A story to share: Matthew 14:13-21

The loaves and fishes

Ask the children if they have ever been really hungry. What does it feel like to be hungry?

When, where have they felt like this? Perhaps on an outing.

One day Jesus went out into the countryside to have a bit of quiet time for himself. When the people in the towns round about heard that Jesus was out in the countryside they set out to find him. Some of them walked many miles to find him. Some brought sick people with them for Jesus to heal.

The day passed quickly and the sun began to set. Soon it would be quite dark. The friends of Jesus came to him and said, 'This is a lonely place and soon it will be night. Send the people away, into the towns and villages to buy themselves some food.' Jesus replied, 'There is no need for them to go; give them something to eat yourselves.' Jesus' friends answered, 'All we have with us is five loaves and two fish'. 'Bring what you have to me,' said Jesus. Then he told everybody to sit down on the grass. He took the bread and the fishes and blessed them. He broke the loaves up and handed them to his friends to share with the crowds of people. Everybody had plenty to eat and twelve baskets of scraps were left over.

What do the children think this story is about?

Who looked after the people?

Who helped Jesus to care for the hungry people?

How did they help?

Did the friends of Jesus go without food because they gave away what they had?

Who looked after them?

Jesus will always look after us. If we share generously what we have with Jesus, he will always take care of us and give us a lot more than we give him.

Invite the children to sit quietly and think about the story.

Pray the 'Our Father'.

73

A story to share: Luke 10:30-32

The good Samaritan

Ask the children if they have ever been hurt or ill, and who helped them and looked after them.

Have they ever helped or looked after anyone?

Once upon a time, a long time ago, a man was travelling from Jerusalem to Jericho when a gang of robbers attacked him. They stole everything he had – probably his horse, his money, his clothes, everything. Then they beat him up and ran off, leaving him almost dead by the side of the road.

Some time later a priest came travelling down the same road. He saw the man lying by the roadside, but he did not stop. Next a lawyer came along the road. He too saw the injured man lying in the gutter, but he did not stop either. Then along the road came a man from Samaria. He saw the injured man and was full of pity for him. He went up to the man, bandaged his wounds, and lifted him onto his own horse. He took him to an inn where he stayed with the injured man and looked after him. Next day he gave the innkeeper some money and said, 'Look after this man until I return. On my way back I will give you more money if you have to spend extra.'

Of the three travellers, who do you think was a true friend to the injured man?

Jesus is the man who always stops to help. He would never walk past anyone in need. We can always trust Jesus. He will always be there for us. On the cross he gave his own life for us.

A story to share: John 3:4-17

Jesus washes his disciples' feet

Have a bowl, a jug of water, some towels and a picture of Jesus with you.

Are the children given help with washing themselves?

When? By whom?

While his friends were at supper, Jesus got up from the table, wrapped a towel round his waist and, taking a bowl, he poured water into it from a jug. Then he knelt down and began to wash the feet of his friends and to wipe them with the towel he was wearing. He came to Simon Peter, who asked him, 'Lord, are you going to wash my feet?'

Jesus said to him, 'Now you do not understand what I am doing, but later you will understand.'

'Never, you will never wash my feet,' said Peter. Jesus replied, 'If I do not wash you, you can share nothing with me.'

'Then wash not only my feet but my hands and head as well, Lord,' replied Peter.

'You do not need washing all over if you have had a bath,' said Jesus. 'You are clean.'

Then Jesus said, 'Do you understand what I have done to you? If I, your Lord, have washed your feet, you should wash each other's feet. I have given you an example so that you may copy what I have done for you.'

Is Jesus telling us that we should go around washing each other's feet?

What is Jesus really showing us here?

Jesus wants us to be like him. What is Jesus really like?

Invite the children to reflect quietly on what Jesus is like for them. Perhaps they could share their thoughts with the group.

In what ways can we be like Jesus?

Unit 4: Celebration

Parents' and catechists' notes

Celebration is inseparable from life. It helps us to let go of the past, accept the present and move into the future. The needs of every age are met in celebration, from the youngest child enthralled by Christmas lights, to the most senior among us, seeing the present with the eyes of memory and life experience as well as anew through the eyes of the young.

Every family has its own special days and occasions; days on which they celebrate the love and joy they share with one another as well as the times in which perhaps they have supported each other through sorrow; events marking life's milestones, the birth of a baby, starting school, becoming a teenager and many more.

As Christians, liturgical celebration is the heartbeat of our lives, illuminating, giving meaning, direction and new impetus to our everyday lives as, week by week, we respond to the invitation to celebrate the Lord's day with the other members of our Christian family.

Throughout the year, as we celebrate the seasons, feast days and festivals of the Church, children gradually come to know and begin to understand the great stories of God's love for us and how Jesus redeems us.

On the Lord's day we Christians respond to Christ's invitation to celebrate our birth to new life begun in baptism and fed in the Eucharist. From celebration to celebration we proclaim the death of the Lord until he comes in glory, as we journey through this life to the celebration of the heavenly banquet where we will celebrate forever at the table of the Lord.

> It was above all on 'the first day of the week', Sunday, the day of Jesus' resurrection, that the Christians met 'to break bread'. From that time on, down to our own day, the celebration of the Eucharist has been continued, and remains the centre of the Church's life. 1343

When we celebrate the memorial of his sacrifice we carry out the command Our Lord gave the night before he died, 'Do this in remembrance of me'. In doing so, we offer to God the gifts of creation, bread and wine, given to us by God and which, by the power of the Holy Spirit and the words of Christ, become the body and blood of Christ. In this way Christ is really and mysteriously made present.

The Eucharist is a celebration of:

- thanksgiving and praise to God;
- the sacrificial memorial of Christ and his Body;
- the presence of Christ by the power of his Word and of his Spirit. 1358

Group session 6: Celebration

Find out what the children understand by 'celebration'.

What do we do when we celebrate a birthday, for example? How do we make the day special; honour someone? Encourage the children to give other examples of celebration and to explain why particular events are celebrated.

◆ Page 18: We celebrate at home

Invite the children to describe some of the special days they celebrate with their families at home. Which family celebration is their favourite and why?

Children complete page 18 at home.

◆ Page 19: We celebrate at church

Invite the children to describe some of the special days they celebrate with God's family at church. Which church celebration is their favourite and why?

Complete page 19. Help the children to fill in a liturgical celebration for each month of the year.

Every weekend Jesus invites us, his family, to a special celebration. We gather with God's family in church. We call this special celebration the Mass.

At Mass we give God praise, honour and thanks. We rejoice in Jesus' love for us, the love of Jesus which lights up the world. We remember how, in baptism, we were called to be children of the light. As God's family we share the light and joy of Jesus with everyone we meet.

◆ Page 21: This year will be a year of special celebration. This year will be the children's first celebration of communion.

Home session 6: Celebration

With your child talk about days which are special to your family, such as birthdays, baptisms, anniversaries, Mothers' Day, Fathers' Day, Christmas, Easter.

Which family celebration is your child's favourite? Why?

◆ On page 18 help your child to fill in special days your family celebrates, against the months.

With your child look at the list of special days we celebrate at church, shown on page 19. Tell your child what is celebrated on these days, You may be able to find pictures which illustrate some of the feasts and festivals.

◆ On page 20 help your child to make a page of celebration.

Look out old invitations, birthday cards with pictures of people at parties, Christmas cards or magazine illustrations.

◆ The invitation on page 21 is very important. Explain to your child that this is a personal invitation from Jesus. Help your child to fill in their name, put in a photograph of themselves, and colour the invitation in. Tell them how they are preparing for their special day of celebration when they will receive Jesus in Holy Communion.

Unit 5: Remembering

Parents' and catechists' notes

While they were at supper, he took bread, said the blessing, broke the bread and gave it to his disciples, saying: 'Take this, all of you, and eat it: this is my body which will be given up for you.'

In the same way, he took the cup, filled with wine.

He gave you thanks, and, giving the cup to his disciples, said: 'Take this, all of you, and drink from it: this is the cup of my blood, the blood of the new and everlasting covenant. It will be shed for you and for all men so that sins may be forgiven. Do this in memory of me.'

From the English translation of The Missal.

At the Last Supper, on the night he was betrayed, our Saviour instituted the eucharistic sacrifice of his body and blood.

By celebrating the Last Supper with the disciples in the course of the Passover meal, Jesus gave the Jewish Passover its definitive meaning. Jesus' passing over to his Father by his death and resurrection, the new Passover, is anticipated in the Supper and celebrated in the Eucharist, which fulfils the Jewish Passover and anticipates the final Passover of the Church in the glory of the Kingdom. 1340

The Eucharist is the heart of our faith. The inexhaustible richness of the Eucharist is expressed in the many names given to this sacrament down the centuries, each name emphasising a different aspect of the mystery.

Because it is an action of thanksgiving to God it is named 'Eucharist' from the Greek words eucharistein and eulogein, recalling Jewish blessings, especially during a meal, which proclaim the wonder of God's works: creation, redemption and sanctification. 1328-29

Remembering the meal Jesus shared with his disciples on the eve of his passion, we use the name the Lord's Supper to describe the Eucharist.

In the early Church the first Christians gathered for the 'Breaking of Bread'. As part of a Jewish meal, when at table with his friends, Jesus blessed, broke and distributed the bread. Also, after his resurrection, his friends recognised him at 'the breaking of bread'. For the early Christians, to eat the broken bread of Christ was to enter into communion with him and to form one body with him. 1329

The sacrament is also called the memorial of the Lord's Passion and Resurrection. Our Christian liturgy not only recalls the events that saved us, but actualises them, makes them present. The paschal mystery of Christ is celebrated, not repeated. It is the celebrations that are repeated. In each celebration there is an outpouring of the Holy Spirit that makes the unique mystery present.

You ask how the bread becomes the Body of Christ and the wine his Blood . . . the Holy Spirit comes upon them and accomplishes what surpasses every word and thought.

St John Damascene, De fide orthodoxa. 1106

We carry out the command of the Lord by celebrating the memorial of his sacrifice. In so doing, we offer to God the gifts given to us by God, gifts of creation, bread and wine, which, by the power of the Holy Spirit and the words of Christ, have become the body and blood of Christ. Christ is thus really and mysteriously made present. 1357

The name 'Holy Sacrifice' is given because this sacrament makes present the one sacrifice of Christ the Saviour and includes the Church's offering. We use the terms holy sacrifice of the Mass, sacrifice of praise, spiritual sacrifice. 1330

Finally, we call this meal the Holy Mass, Missa, because the liturgy in which the mystery of our salvation is accomplished concludes with a sending forth of the faithful, missio, so that they may fulfil God's will in their daily lives. 1332

Group session 7:
We give God thanks and praise

Materials: selection of pictures illustrating God's
              wonderful world

              glue

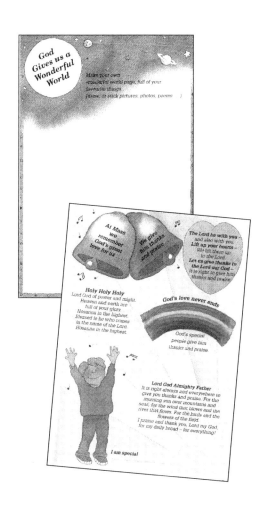

◆ Page 24: God gives us a wonderful world

Invite the children to choose a picture to put on the 'God's Wonderful World' page in their books.

At Mass we remember God's great love for us and the gift of God's wonderful world. We give God thanks and praise.

◆ On page 25, pray the prayer, 'The Lord be with you' with the children, from the heart shape.

Ask the children why they think this prayer is written in a heart shape.

Could they write a prayer on their 'Wonderful World' page to thank God with all their heart?

What would they most like to say thank you for in their prayer?

Read the prayer 'Lord God Almighty Father' from the bottom of page 25.

When we say this great 'Thank You' prayer at Mass, all the angels and saints in heaven join in with us and together we all sing: 'Holy, holy, holy . . .'

Sing a Sanctus known to the group.

To conclude the session, gather everyone together.

Light a candle.

All stand.

Leader: The Lord be with you.

All: And also with you,

Leader: Lift up your hearts.

All: (raising arms) We lift them up to the Lord.

Leader: Let us give thanks to the Lord our God.

All: It is right to give God thanks and praise.

All: Lord God, Almighty Father,

It is right always and everywhere

to give you thanks and praise.

For the morning sun over mountains and seas:

for the wind that blows and the river that flows:

for the birds and the flowers of the field.

We praise and thank you, Lord our God,

for our daily bread, for everything,

as, together with all the angels and the saints,

we sing:'Holy, holy, holy . . .' (sung).

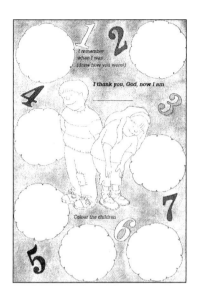

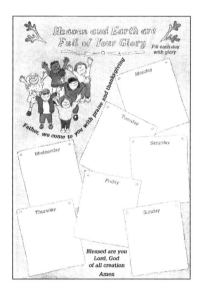

Home session 7: Heaven and earth are full of God's glory

◆ Page 23: I remember when I was . . .

Help the children to find a memory for each year in their lives, for example:

the year they were baptised

the year they received the sacrament of Reconciliation

the year they lost their baby teeth

the year they started school

maybe they moved house, had a baby brother or sister.

Most of these things happen to us only once, but we remember them, celebrate them and give thanks for them over and over again.

◆ Page 26: Heaven and earth are full of your glory

At the end of each day this week, help your child to reflect on what has been special for them that day and for which they would like to give God thanks and praise.

Fill the calendar sheets in with either writing or drawings.

Group session 8: A special meal

Materials: picture of the Last Supper

        unleavened bread

        watercress

        celery

        salt water

        boiled egg

        lamb bone

        apple, honey, nuts, dates

        cinnamon

        sweet red wine

        chalice

Tell the children the Passover story, the great event which Jewish people remember and celebrate each year with a special meal, the great celebration of freedom.

Each year Jewish people come together to remember and to give God thanks and praise as they celebrate a very special event which took place in the history of their people. It is called the Passover. It commemorates the setting free of the people of Israel from slavery in Egypt. Every year since that night, the Jewish people gather together to remember, to give thanks for, and to celebrate God's gift to them of freedom, at a special meal.

The story of the Passover
Exodus 12:21-34; 37-42

When Jesus was on earth he shared many meals with his friends. Every year he celebrated the feast of Passover with his family and friends. This is a special meal for Jewish people even today. For many years the people of Israel were slaves in Egypt. Moses was chosen by God to help to set them free. God sent the ten plagues to frighten the wicked Pharaoh of Egypt. The tenth plague was to be the death of the first-born son in every house not signed with the blood of the lamb. Eventually the people of Israel were set free after they had sacrificed a lamb and signed their door posts with its blood. This was because the avenging angel spared the homes marked with the blood of the lamb and the first-born son was saved. The Israelites had to leave Egypt very quickly, they did not even have time to wait for their bread to rise so, to this day, in memory of their hasty departure, unleavened bread is still used at Passover. Celery dipped in salt is eaten to remind everyone of the bitterness and tears of slavery. A lamb bone is a reminder of the lamb whose blood marked the door posts of the Israelites. Apples mixed with spices, nuts and dates are a symbol of the bricks and mortar the Israelites made in Egypt. Eggs are a symbol of new life, and wine of joy and celebration.

For Jewish people Passover is a great celebration of freedom.

What was sacrificed by the people of Israel to set them free?

What were they set free from?

Where were they free to go?

When Jesus was a little boy, and as he grew up, he celebrated many Passovers with his family and friends.

◆ Page 22: Invitation to Supper

Celebrate a simple Passover meal.

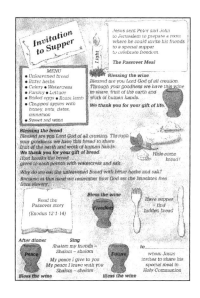

Group session 9:
Through Jesus Christ our Lord

Materials: picture of the Last Supper

              hosts

              chalice

              wine

Jesus celebrated the Last Supper with his friends during a Passover meal.

Tell the story of the Last Supper from Luke 22:7-20.

Invite the children to sit quietly and imagine themselves at the Last Supper.

What can they see happening?

What words can they hear?

At the Last Supper what did Jesus ask us to do to remember him?

What sacrifice did Jesus offer for us?

From what did Jesus' sacrifice set us free?

Where are we free to go now?

With bread and wine, mime the Last Supper with the children.

What did Jesus do with the bread?

What did he say it was?

What did Jesus do with the wine?

What did he say it was?

Jesus died on the cross to give himself for us.

Three days later Jesus rose from the dead and returned to heaven.

Jesus will come again in glory.

When we celebrate the Lord's supper at Mass, the priest says the words of Jesus over the bread and wine:

'Take this, all of you, and eat it: this is my body which will be given up for you . . . This is the cup of my blood, the blood of the new and everlasting covenant. It will be shed for you and for all men so that sins may be forgiven. Do this in memory of me.'

We all respond: 'Christ has died. Christ is risen. Christ will come again.'

Show the children how to receive the hosts and take the chalice and wine.

Explain how we respond 'Amen' to the invitation, 'The body of Christ'. . . 'The blood of Christ'.

Amen. Amen.

◆ Page 28: Through the birth of Jesus, the life of Jesus, the death and resurrection of Jesus, the whole Church on earth and in heaven gives praise and glory to God, united in the Holy Spirit.

We all say AMEN.

◆ Celebrate the 'Breaking of Bread' on page 29.

Home session 8:
Through Jesus Christ our Lord

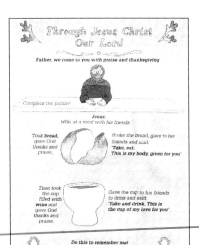

◆ Page 27.

Help your child to draw themselves, your family, their friends seated at the table with Jesus.

Read through the words on this page with your child.

Home session 9: We remember

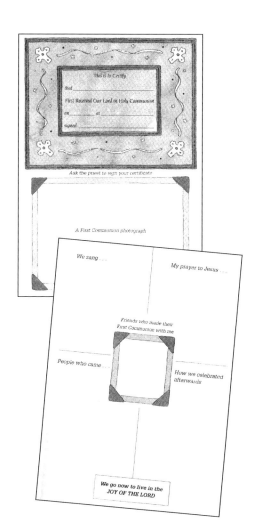

◆ *Pages 30-31: This is to certify . . .*

Help your child to complete their book, 'Meet Christ with Joy', by filling in the communion certificate and having it signed by the priest.

Perhaps have some of the guests at your child's first celebration of communion sign their book.

Fix a photograph of the event on page 30, and help your child fill in the sections of page 31 as a memento of their special day.

Acknowledgements

The publishers wish to express their gratitude to the following for permission to include copyright material in this book:

The Catholic Truth Society, 40-46 Harleyford Road, Vauxhall, London, SE11 5AY, for the extract from '*The Directory on Children's Masses, Code No: Do 459*'.

Geoffrey Chapman, an imprint of Cassell plc, Wellington House, 125 Strand, London, WC2R 0BB, for the extracts from '*The Catechism of the Catholic Church*'. The English translation is © Geoffrey Chapman, an imprint of Cassell plc, and the original Latin text is © Libreria Editrice Vaticana.

Darton, Longman & Todd Ltd, 1 Spencer Court, 140-142 Wandsworth High Street, London, SW18 4JJ, for the Bible quotations which are taken from '*The Jerusalem Bible*' © 1966, 1967 and 1968 Darton, Longman & Todd Ltd and Doubleday & Co. Inc.

Dominican Publications, 42 Parnell Square, Dublin 1, Eire for the extracts from '*Sacrosanctum Concilium*' and '*Dei Verbum 9*'.

The International Commission on English in the Liturgy (ICEL), 1522 K Street, NW, Suite 1000, Washington, DC 20005-1202, USA, for excerpts from the English translation of '*The Roman Missal*' © 1973 International Committee on English in the Liturgy, Inc. All rights reserved.

Every effort has been made to trace copyright owners of material and we hope that no copyright has been infringed. Pardon is sought and apology made if the contrary be the case, and a correction will be made in any reprint of this book.

Printed in the United Kingdom by
Lightning Source UK Ltd., Milton Keynes
136692UK00001BA/5/P